WOLF BOY

WAYLAND
www.waylandbooks.co.uk

First published in 2013 by Wayland

Text copyright © Andrew Fusek Peters 2013
Illustration copyright © Cathy Brett 2013

Wayland
338 Euston Road
London NW1 3BH

Wayland Australia
Level 17/207 Kent Street
Sydney, NSW 2000

The rights of Andrew Fusek Peters to be identified as the Author
and Cathy Brett to be identified as the Illustrator of this Work
have been asserted by them in accordance with the Copyright,
Designs and Patents Act, 1988.

All rights reserved

Series Editor: Louise John
Series design: Robert Walster
Design: Lisa Peacock
Consultant: Fiona Collins

A CIP catalogue record for this book is available
from the British Library.

ISBN 9780750268974

Printed in China

Wayland is a division of Hachette Children's Books,
an Hachette UK Company

www.hachette.co.uk

WOLF BOY

Andrew Fusek Peters
and Cathy Brett

Titles in the series

The Crawling Hand

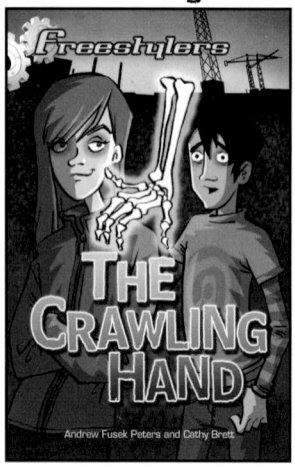

9780750268950

Sliced in Two

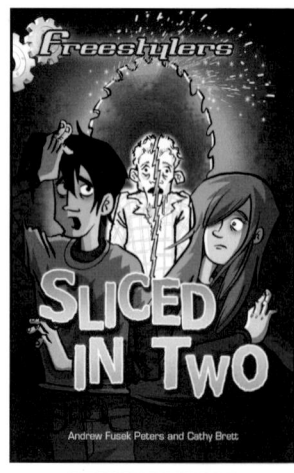

9780750268967

Wolf Boy

9780750268974

High Stakes

9780750268981

CHAPTER 1

I woke up sweating. What was that noise? My bedroom was empty. But there it was again.

"Wooooooh!"

It sounded like a cat being strangled. Hairs stood up on the back of my neck. I jumped out of bed and pulled the window shut. Then I dived under the duvet. Not very safe but worth a try.

WOLF BOY

Next morning, Mrs Benn knocked at the door. Mrs Benn runs the local neighbourhood watch. She doesn't like teenagers. At all.

"I have a case for you, Jas.

Someone's dog must have escaped and it's making too much noise!"

"Yeah, Mrs B," I said, rubbing my eyes. "I heard it."

"Find the dog! Find the owner! Report to me!" Her eyes flashed.

WOLF BOY

She held her clipboard with hands of steel. Mrs Benn was far more scary than a barking dog.

That night, my best friend, Sam, and I went to take a look. Up in the sky, the moon was full and the streets shone like silver.

"I'm not sure about this at all, Sam!"

"But Jas, we need to solve the case!" Sam strode down the narrow street. She peered behind bins and looked under cars.

"Maybe we should call the dog patrol," I said.

"Maybe you should stop moaning!" said Sam. Suddenly she froze.

"What?"

At the end of the alley was a tree. The ground was full of empty beer cans and shadows.

"Look!" Sam hissed.

"It's a tree! Well done, Sam!"

"No. Look properly!"

I took a step forward. There was something in the darkness right in front of us.

It moved slowly out of the shadows. Under the streetlight I saw a mass of fur and huge teeth.

"OMG!" I moaned, as the thing began to growl.

CHAPTER 2

"You poor little thing!" said Sam, holding out her hand.

"Sam! Get back! Your fingers are going to get munched!"

The 'thing' growled. It was like a cat purring, but ten times louder and ten times more scary.

My eyes worked it out. The thing looked like a dog, but much bigger. Red eyes glowed at us. Its teeth dripped saliva.

"We should, like, run!" I hissed.

"Why?"

"Because 'thingy-wingy' is about to have us for din-dins. That's why!"

But the beast did not bite Sam's fingers off. Instead she gently stroked its thick fur. "All you wanted was

17

a scratch, eh?" she said. Then she turned to face me.

"The shop round the corner is still open. Get a couple of steaks, there's a good boy."

My face went red. "I am not a good boy! And I can't leave you alone with that…"

"Lost little doggy?" said Sam. "Don't worry, I'll be fine."

I went off in a sulk.

Sometimes Sam pushed me too far. I got the steaks and came back, waiting to find her chewed into pieces. But the beast was curled up by her feet.

WOLF BOY

Soon as I was close, the beast began to sniff. I put the steaks on the ground and they disappeared in one bite of its massive teeth.

"What next?" I said.

"Well, he's not howling, is he? Mrs Benn will be happy. Job done. Case solved."

"Not really. Face it, Sam. This is no normal pooch."

Before she could answer, a cloud crossed the moon. When it had gone, so had the beast.

CHAPTER 3

It's never a dull moment with me. Last night it was a mad beast. This morning it was a mad kid. There he was, on top of the school roof, about to jump off. And there was Barry Jones, the boy with a single brain cell, shouting up at him.

"Come on, Wolf Boy. You know you want to jump!" His two mates were by his side, grunting.

The kid himself stood on the edge

of the roof. Hard to see what he looked like under all his hair. He needed a haircut. For a second, he looked at me. Red eyes. Strange. Where had I seen him before?

Just then, Sam came running round

the corner. "Well done, Barry!" she shouted.

"You what?" he asked.

"I always knew you were stupid, Barry Jones. Now, you've proved it. If that poor kid jumps and breaks his leg, it'll be your fault!"

Barry put up his fist.

"Oh! Now you're going to punch a girl. What a brave boy you are!" Sam sneered.

"You…" Barry was lost for words. He put down his fist and slunk away.

A few minutes later the boy was back down on the ground.

"Are you OK?" I asked.

"Guess so," said the boy. "Tired. It's all too much."

"What is?"

WOLF BOY

"I keep waking up in strange places. Must be sleepwalking. Dad doesn't care. He's too busy working. Barry Jones doesn't help."

Sam was staring at the boy.

"Look!" she hissed.

"What?"

There was a label hanging out of the boy's pocket.

The boy shrugged. "Found it when I woke up this morning."

The label was for a pack of fresh steak.

Sam and I looked at each other. "No way!" I said.

CHAPTER 4

"But that means…" Sam said.

"Yeah. And it seems like he doesn't know." I looked at the kid. How could I break the news?

"Listen kid, what year are you in?"

"Year seven," said the boy. "It's not

my fault I'm small. That's why Barry picks on me."

"Right," I said. "Barry Jones is a coward. He wouldn't pick on someone his own size. So, I've got some bad news and some good news. Which do you want first?"

The boy looked at Sam and then at Jas. "The bad news, I think."

"OK. Here goes. You know that full moon last night?"

"Yes?"

"Do you wonder why you feel a bit

odd on the full moon?"

"Not really, but I get shivery, then sleepy. Next thing I know, I'm waking up somewhere miles from home."

"Right," I said. "That's because…"

"… you're a werewolf!" finished Sam.

WOLF BOY

The boy burst out laughing. "Oh great, I've been saved from the bullies by a couple of nutters!"

"The steak label in your pocket. We fed you last night."

The boy frowned. "I think I can

remember. I was howling. I felt scared…"

"Yeah, you were keeping us all awake!" I said. "If Mrs Benn gets hold of you, you'll be locked up."

"Who is Mrs Benn?"

"Never mind," said Sam, "The point is, you know you are a werewolf. That's the first step…"

"So, I grow all hairy, run around

howling and that's that?" The boy was almost crying now.

"No," Sam said. "Just trust me and we'll sort out that bully Barry Jones."

"Yup," I said. "We just wait for the next full moon. Your job for now is to keep out of Barry's way."

CHAPTER 5

The month went by quickly. No more noisy nights. Mrs Benn was smiling. Until the next full moon.

It was a good one, round and fat as a spinning coin. Wolf Boy was with us. One second we were chatting with a twelve-year-old kid. The next second, there was a huge beast growling at us.

"What if he gets us?" I hissed.

"Grow up!" said Sam. "It's not you he's angry with."

A bit of spying had given us the info we needed. Barry and his mates hung out round the skate park after dark. Time for a little visit.

Half an hour later, I climbed over the gates. "Hey, Barry!" I shouted.

"Found another brain cell yet?"

Barry turned round. With his mates as back-up, he came towards me. "You are so dead, Jas."

At that moment, a great howl filled the sky.

WOLF BOY

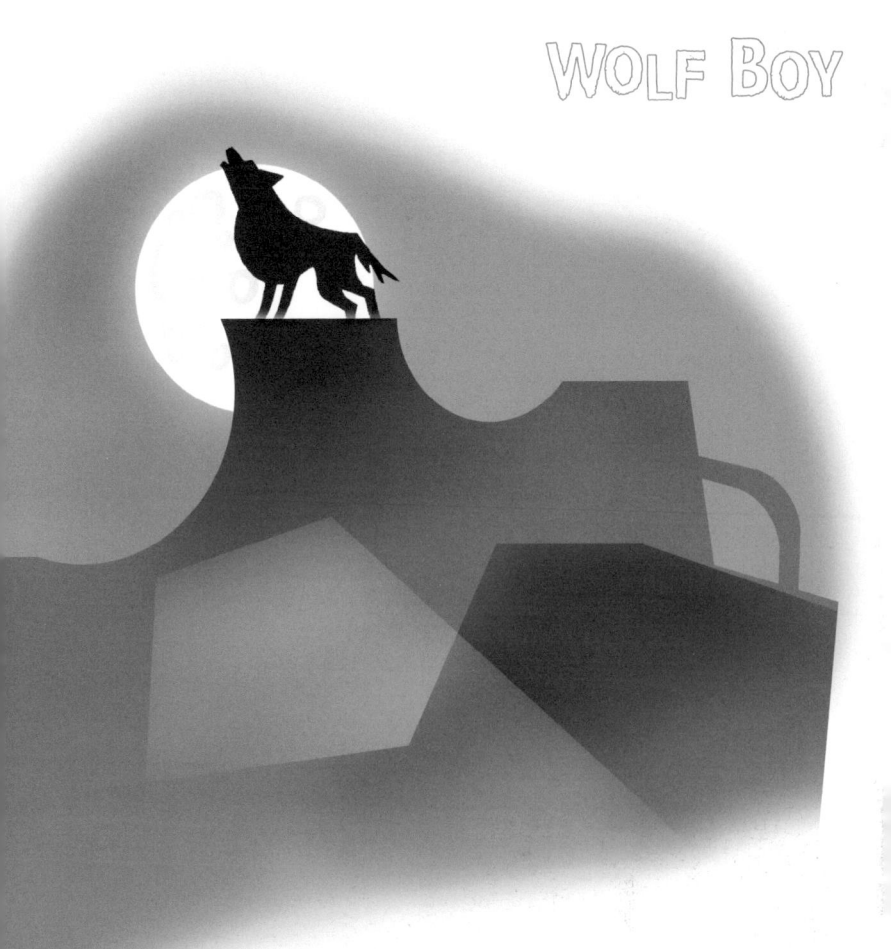

"What's that?" shouted one of Barry's mates.

"Sounds like a mad dog!" said the other, shaking.

"Don't be a wimp!" Barry snarled.

"Get him!" he pointed at me.
His mates came towards me, fists in the air.

Everything slowed down. The moon had turned the skate park white – the bowl, the grind rails, the ramp.

And there was Wolf Boy, huge and terrifying. His jaws drooled and his eyes burned red as he leaped straight towards Barry.

Barry froze to the spot. "Help!" he shouted, then turned and ran.

Sam came up behind me. "Good dog!" she said to Wolf Boy, who sat down and wagged his tail. "Steak for tea, I think!"

Later that night we stood at the edge of the zoo. Wolf Boy howled and nearly jumped out of his skin, when he heard the wolves howl back. He jumped over the fence to hang out with them. Wolf Boy was happy and the bullies were history.

I never got paid by Mrs Benn, but in my eyes, the case was solved.

FOR TEACHERS

About Freestylers

Freestylers is a series of carefully levelled stories, especially geared for struggling readers of both sexes. With very low reading age and high interest age, these books are humorous, fun, up-to-the-minute and edgy. Core characters provide familiarity in all of the stories, build confidence and ease pupils from one story through to the next, accelerating reading progress.

Freestylers can be used for both guided and independent reading. To make the most of the books you can:

• Focus on making each reading session successful. Talk about the text before the pupil starts reading. Introduce the characters, the storyline and any unfamiliar vocabulary.

• Encourage the pupil to talk about the book during reading and after reading. How would they have felt if they were Jas? Or Sam? How would they have gone about solving the mystery?

• Talk about which parts of the story they like best and why.

For guidance, this story has been approximately measured to:

National Curriculum Level: 2A
Reading Age: 6
Book Band: White

ATOS: 2.4
Lexile ® Measure [confirmed]: 340L